Crescendo Publishing Presents

Instant Insights on...

EMPOWERMENT

12 Leadership Powers *for* Successful Women

Sylvia Becker-Hill

small guides. BIG IMPACT.

Instant Insights on...

12 Leadership Powers for Successful Women
By Sylvia Becker-Hill

ISBN: 978-1-944177-39-3 (p)
ISBN: 978-1-944177-40-9 (e)

Crescendo Publishing, LLC
300 Carlsbad Village Drive
Ste. 108A, #443
Carlsbad, California 92008-2999

www.CrescendoPublishing.com
GetPublished@CrescendoPublishing.com

What You'll Learn in this Book

Despite the fact that female leaders are on the rise in corporations, as business owners, as heads of nonprofit organizations, and as national government leaders, less than 10 percent of leadership books being published are written by women for women. Concepts of leadership and power are still considered "male topics." *Instant Insights on 12 Leadership Powers for Successful Women*, by Sylvia Becker-Hill closes that gap.

Focusing on the powers that turn women into powerful, successful, results-producing leaders, she puts together a curriculum that reads like the "Hogwarts School of Leadership for Women," twelve powers that leave the unhealthy paradigm of perfectionistic, stressed-out super women behind us and call forth the new dawn of Über Women, the leaders of tomorrow.

Each chapter starts with a different power statement that readers can use to rewire their brain through the power of daily repetition. Each chapter ends with three Instant Insights into the categories of knowing, trusting, and leading.

Instant Insights on 12 Leadership Powers for Successful Women, is written to give professional women a clear blueprint for what it means to be a powerful Über Woman, ready to shape the future.

In this book, you'll get **Instant Insights** on…

- How to stay motivated in business or career when things get tough
- How to turn fears and self-sabotage into resilience and determination
- How to work and live drama-free
- How to create exquisite self-care for a healthy, sexy, gracefully aging body
- How to make decisions fast without regrets
- How to use emotions productively while keeping your cool
- How to lead with power and love

A Gift from the Author

Enhance your reading experience and make your implementation of the *Instant Insights* into your leadership practice easier with a bundle of self-coaching tools I'm sure you'll love. Use them daily for a minimum of thirty days, and you will experience sustainable change. Enjoy feeling more and more like a true successful Über Woman leader.

You'll find details on how to use these self-coaching tools on the same page as the download link itself. Get immediate access to all the gifts as digital downloads behind this link:

http://www.ueberwomen.com/instant-insights-gifts.html

Here is what I've created for you:

- A beautifully designed poster to print and use for the daily practice with the twelve power statements.

- A relaxing audio created to empower and support you in implementing each of the Uber Woman Power Statements listed throughout this book.

Table of Contents

Dedication

To all my wonderful women mentors who modeled pieces of authentic female leadership for me.

To all my wonderful female executive clients that I had the honor to help break through glass ceilings inside their corporations and between their ears.

To all my female business owner clients I helped to become leaders not only of their own business but of their whole life.

To my mom who showed me that there is no greater power than unconditional love.

To my new readers:
Uncaged Unleashed Unashamed Unstoppable Über Women, the female leaders of tomorrow!

Introduction

We are living during exciting times of global evolutionary changes! After a century of women fighting for equal rights with men, more women are in leading roles inside corporations, running their own businesses, leading nonprofits, and governing whole nations than ever before. We are still around 30 percent away from a 50:50 share of governance, which would reflect the simple fact that women make up half of human kind, yet all evolutionary trends point in the same positive direction: true partnership between men and woman.

Women's evolution unfolded through stages in the last 100 years. The first stage was "Wonder Woman," an idealized figure who functioned like a projection screen in film, media, and art, capable of whatever society at that time needed without a true reflection in reality. The second stage was "super women." Since the eighties, women first needed to become more male than their male peers, including wearing shoulder pads in business suits, mimicking male bodies in order to fit in, until they finally drowned in the nineties under perfectionism and the pressure to have it all. They paid a high price: stress, denial of their often different views and values, and the loss of femininity, integrity, and sadly often health.

The good news is that a new breed of female leaders is emerging, women who define their own way of leading, working, and living; women who bring back their original feminine authenticity, intuition, spirituality, and perspectives into the world. I label these women at the dawn of evolution's next era "Über Women," from the German word "über," which means "one of its kind, fertile, and abundant."

The world needs more Über Women in all sections of society, yet there is not a lot of leadership education available before women reach relatively high ranks in the corporate world. The few opportunities offered were all based on a definition of leadership that assumed leadership is male. Of all the books ever written about leadership, 90 percent are written by men for men, analyzing male leadership examples. The few books about powerful female leadership are either autobiographic, like the recent controversial best seller from Sheryl Sandberg, *Lean in*, or they are highly academic in style and volume like *The Rise of the Female Executive: How Women's Leadership is Accelerating Cultural Change*, written by Peninah Thomson, Tom Lloyd, and Clare Laurent.

There seems to be no easy-to-read, practical book for women to learn what makes a woman a powerful leader: an **Über** Woman!

The book you are holding closes that gap. I wrote this book based on my experience as an executive change strategist and coach for female leaders gained over eighteen years, as I analyzed their success patterns and researched leadership definitions, models, and paradigms in management literature. For nearly two decades I have been asking female leaders: "From the powers you learned through the coaching process with me, which are the most important ones bringing the results you want?"

My clients' answers created the backbone to the Twelve **Über** Women Powers you hold in your hands. It's a curriculum written with the intention of helping you discover the different powers you already may have or know now you need to develop, so that you can understand them and become inspired to train and apply them beyond this book in your work and private life. It's the

"Hogwarts School of Women's Leadership" in the size of a small pocketbook. Don't underestimate its power to change your life!

The Power of Total Alignment

Über Woman Power Statement:
"I align my brain for success and my life with my purpose."

You are intelligent. You know what you want. You made a plan, decided on a strategy, and executed it to the best of your abilities, yet your desired results are not there. You feel frustrated and a bit at a loss not knowing what to do differently. When life feels hard and we have to push ourselves through some kind of "fog of resistance" engulfing us, that indicates a lack of alignment.

What is alignment? Alignment is created by directing different things toward the same endpoint or focus, arranging things in a straight line. Alignment is also known to create more strengths, brightness, and power. The difference that makes a laser brighter and able to singularly focus on a tiny spot compared to an ordinary lightbulb is the alignment of the wavelengths of the light it's emanating.

We are not just one thing. We consist of different parts that all together make us "us" and unique. In our brain we have our conscious and subconscious mind, which often are not aligned. Consciously you might pursue the goal to ask for a higher salary next time you have a review conversation with your boss, yet your subconscious mind has a strong loyalty program running that says, "You are not allowed to outshine your bigger sister" or "Your parents were poor. Affirm their life was a good life by staying poor yourself." So every time you consciously want to start a conversation about a higher salary (or you are a businesswoman who consciously decided to up-level her fee structure), your subconscious mind starts sabotaging you according to its programming by making you sweat, stumble, and ask with a shaky voice for lower numbers than you had planned.

Another area of misalignment is our own inner values. Values function like a compass. They give us our own personal "true north." They talk to us in hunches, whispers, and intuition. They are like guiding posts showing us the direction to go next. We all have a cocktail of different values inside us. These values come from early childhood programming through our parents, family environment, cultural imprints, religious indoctrination, political viewpoints of the adults around us, and more. Most of the time they form some kind of hierarchy with one or two values at the top.

Let's say as a professional woman you have "financial independence" as one of your top values, and you set out to define goals for your career or business accordingly. Maybe you plan to launch a new product line that promises big revenues or step up to the director level of your corporation with a big jump on the salary scale. Yet another one of your top values is "health and fitness." Launching a new product line and stepping into the director position might mean you will have less time for sports. Finding the time for massages or true relaxation doing nothing seems impossible. This is a classic internal value conflict that will show as external resistance to your set goals.

As women, we naturally fill a wide range of different roles. We are business owners or executives, wives/spouses, mothers, daughters, colleagues, girlfriends, sisters, PTA members, housewives, social-life organizers for the whole family, homework supervisors, pet caregivers, grandparent caregivers, volunteers at school, volunteers at church and in the community, and so on and on. It's very easy to see conflicts and misalignment arise between these different roles. The most classic one is between "career woman" and "mother."

To be a successful leader, you have to set time aside to learn about yourself by asking yourself these questions: What are my conscious desires? What goals do I choose to pursue? What gets stirred up when I put my attention on my goals? Fears? Resistances? What is important for me in life? What red flags warn me that I am in danger of hurting myself by compromising an important value? How good is my time and energy management when it comes to juggling all my different roles? How clear and strong am I in setting healthy boundaries between my roles and duties?

Alignment among the different parts that make you "you" is not easy, yet it is possible. It becomes easier and easier the clearer your foundation of self-awareness is and as you set more healthy habits and supporting structures in place.

One hundred percent alignment attracts the right supporters and resources and generates synchronicities that make acting so effortless that the resulting success feels magical! An aligned leader is a successful leader!

Your Instant Insights...

- Know that resistance, struggles, and lack of desired results are indicators of a lack of alignment.

- Trust that when you do your inner alignment work between your conscious and subconscious mind, your inner values and your active roles, your outer life will mirror your inner alignment.

- Lead from alignment among all your parts, and enjoy seeing yourself reaping results beyond what seemed possible before.

The Power of Purpose

Über Woman Power Statement:
"I focus on my biggest 'Why' at all times."

Motivation comes from movement. As a leader, you have to move yourself every day from the moment the alarm clock rings. Where is the motivation for this constant movement coming from?

From a brain's perspective, there are only two human drivers: away from pain and toward pleasure. Both pulls—even though seemingly opponents—work hand in hand. When you want to lose weight, you are moving away from the pain you feel when looking in the mirror and judging your belly as ugly and yourself as undisciplined, while at the same time you are moving yourself toward the joy of fitting back into the dress you wore on your first date with your husband fifteen years ago before you had kids.

External pressure and "should-ing" oneself to do anything works only short term. For big changes and big goals in life, you need resilience and stamina. Professional women like you are often ambitious. They want more from life. They want to be challenged, and they want to grow, to live their full potential. For this, stepping again and again out of your comfort zone must become a daily practice, yet here we are hitting against a hardwired bias in our own brain! Leaving the old known comfort zone feels painful for the brain. It does everything in its power to stop us with a wide range of tricks like distraction, becoming sick, or producing dramas. In order to override the "away from pain" tendencies of our brain, we have to have a big "why," a purpose, a calling that brings us huge pleasure when we imagine its fulfillment pulling us through when it gets tough.

What is your big "why"?

My purpose in life is to heal the pain of disconnect on this planet by fostering the next phase of evolution of true partnership between men and women. I do this through my business mission of empowering women to be fully realized leaders who have it all without the usual sacrifices. I needed years to become clear about all that, yet it was right under my nose. It was Steve Jobs who made the idea famous that we can't connect the dots of our life looking forward into our future, yet we can when we look back and analyze our past.

What if your whole life is like a treasure map that constantly gives you clues regarding your talents, your strengths, and your perfect makeup for your perfect mission to fulfill in this lifetime? What if nothing you ever experienced was just an accident? What if every job you had, every partnership, every success, and every failure prepared you for your ultimate mission in life? What if you don't need anyone else to tell you what to do? What if all answers are mapped out by your own life?

An Über Woman who knows herself and why she does what she does is like a warrior who can't get distracted by drama or unimportant things other people throw into her space. An Über Woman who is clear about her purpose can easily say "No!" to the wrong invitations because she had already powerfully said "Yes!" to her "true north."When you have a burning passion and commitment for your purpose it becomes easy to set boundaries and stop the epidemic of a woman's curse to attempt to please everyone.

Being clear about your big "why" makes alignment of your different parts effortless. Your big "why" puts the sparkle in your eyes, which makes you irresistible to supporters, lovers, or clients. A woman fulfilled by this inner knowing has charisma and power. The "what" unfolds logically, and the "how" is being cared for by others. Focus on your purpose—always—and you cannot show up as less than a powerful leader!

Your Instant Insights...

- Know: People focus too much on the "what," worry too much about the "how," and forget their big "why."

- Trust: When looked back without judgment, your own life gives you all the clues to define your personal big "why."

- Lead by starting each day with connecting to your big "why," which ensures positive attitude, clarity of direction, and motivation to act.

The Power of Free Attention

Über Woman Power Statement:
"I am my word and keep my integrity strong."

As a leader, you are pursuing goals you can't accomplish alone. You need your team, employees, followers, or tribe to work for you, to help you align behind you and your vision. How do you do that? When you analyze the success of powerful leaders, you will find that they all master what I call the "art of attention management." Attention is the brain energy people exude when they focus on something. People's aligned attention on a shared goal makes them unstoppable! In order to lead and guide other people's attention, understand (a) what it is and how it works, and (b) how to manage your own attention, gaining as much of it as possible!

Have you ever felt the hair on the back of your neck stand up and you turned around because you felt that someone was watching you from behind? What you were sensing from that person was literally their attention beam on you! If you are reading this book right now in a public place, put it down and play with your attention. Focus on this book in your lap, and then look up and focus on someone close by from behind. Do that strongly and see if you can make them turn around!

Attention is one of our most important resources to get anything done. Attention is so powerful that some scientists say, "We are where our attention is." Have you ever spoken to a person who, despite the fact that they were sitting right in front of you, was not "there"? It's the state when we say, "Hey, are you listening? You seem absentminded ..."

Look up again from the book and gaze around. Can you see by watching and observing other people where their attention is? That is a hugely important skill for any leader! When you can sense where people's attention is, you can connect with them by addressing their point of focus by talking about it, and then—when you can clearly feel you both "clicked"—you can move their attention in the direction of your desired focus. That is called "pacing and leading."

Attention is a brain resource that sadly gets easily drained. When we have too much to do, when we multitask, when we are stressed, running late, tired, or scared, our attention gets drained faster than when we are refreshed, relaxed, and focused deliberately on just one thing. Attention comes in two different forms: neutral and charged. Neutral attention is equal to free attention. It is at our disposal, and we can decide where to move it and/or what to focus on. For you as a leader, it is crucial to have as much as possible of this kind of attention—free and under your control. Sadly, we all get easily triggered to add charge to our attention through two impulses in our brain: desire ("I like that! I want that!") or repulsion ("I don't like that! I hate that!"). As soon we feel either attraction or aversion regarding something, we charge the related attention. If the emotion is very big, the charge gets so strong that it fixes a huge part or all our attention!

Imagine you are sitting in an important meeting and you have to present something, yet you had a terrible, sleepless night after a fight with your spouse who told you they want a divorce, or right before the meeting you got a phone call from a family member telling you your mother has stage 4 cancer. Where will your attention be? On the meeting you are in or on the private matters that disturb you? Even something positive, like a dream vacation that's supposed to start in the afternoon, can make it impossible to keep your attention where you are in the morning! When your company goes through a big restructuring process and your staff is in fear that a lot of them might lose their jobs, where do you think their attention is when you want to start brainstorming about a new product launch?

Your goal has to be to free up any fixed attention you have in your life and make it easy for your team members to have lots of free attention to help you. Here is a powerful exercise for you: brainstorm a list about every big or small thing in your life that you sense you have fixed attention on. When you are honest and if you have never done a list like that, you should come up with sixty to a hundred items!

After you make the list, write behind each item one of the following three capital letters: A, standing for "Here is action needed," or B, standing for "Here is communication needed," or C, standing for "This is outdated, can't be fixed any longer, and I declare it officially complete." Write everything that got a C on a new sheet of paper. Read the list out loud and then say out loud, "I, (your name), declare all these items on this list complete. I choose to stop giving them any attention any longer." And then you burn that piece of paper in a safe way.

Category A items are often things like a postponed dentist appointment, car checkup, repairing the dripping faucet in the kitchen, buying a new filter for the fridge, creating the manual for project X, and creating with your assistant a new e-mail folder system. Category B items are typically avoided communications like calling your grandmother, writing a thank-you card, calling someone you hurt and who deserves an apology, or talking to a team member about a conflict. Choose one item each day from both category A and B and simply get them done. You will be amazed by how much more energy you will feel, what a great confidence boost that process brings, and how much easier your role as a leader becomes!

Your Instant Insights...

- Know: What you give attention, grows.
- Trust: Strong emotional charge, negative or positive, fixates attention and drains you.
- Lead with free attention, and you will have more energy to produce your desired results.

The Power of Ego-Love

Über Woman Power Statement:
"I team with my ego and turn my fears into fuel."

When most people think about the ego, they think about extremely confident people; mean, aggressive people; or attention-seeking people. The word "egocentric" is a negative judgment about someone who is "too full of him or herself." There is a lot of debate in the media about how much of an ego a leader needs in order to be successful in today's demanding corporate or economic environments and whether too much ego is detrimental for a company's culture—or might even tempt the leader to step beyond the line of integrity or even the law. Wherever you look, all articles and conversations have one thing in common about the ego: they are all negative! The ego needs to be restrained, limited, kept at bay.

What if this is the wrong approach? What if this completely misses the point about what the ego is and how best to utilize it as a female leader?

In my understanding, the ego is the part of your subconscious mind committed to your safety and survival. It gets developed and programmed during your very early childhood years before your more mature conscious mind in your neocortex develops. The ego ensures your survival. For example, when you, as a three-year-old, put your hand over an open fire and it hurts, it's the ego that makes you pull your hand quickly away and prevents you from getting burned. When you are standing in front of your preschool class singing a kids' song and everyone starts laughing because you mixed up the lyrics, it is your ego that promises you that it will do all in its mighty power to protect you from this social embarrassment happening again. When your mom cries after a conflict with your dad over money and she talks with you about budgets and why you can't get the big new bike you wanted and why they had to cancel the vacation trip, it is your ego that promises you it will do what is in its power to make sure you will never fail to get something because of a lack of money and that you will never hurt your parents' feelings by outshining them by becoming wealthier than they were.

All those programs, vows, and beliefs from our early childhood are deeply ingrained in our subconscious mind. It is our job through introspection, coaching, or therapy to heal, integrate, and rewire them. Otherwise, they get triggered when we are adults, make us regress into little girls, and sabotage our successes as female leaders! For example, when a perfectly prepared, brilliant, mature woman starts to sweat and stumbles while speaking in public, it's her ego kicking in, trying to keep her safe from the social embarrassment she experienced as a four-year-old! Or when a mature woman struggles to pay off her credit-card debts, maybe it's her ego sabotaging it, keeping the old programming running to never allow a wish not granted because of a lack of money. Or when a businesswoman shies away from asking for higher fees or a corporate woman accepts a salary that is way too low, it might be their egos protecting them from outshining a loved one by making more money.

The point is that your ego is not your enemy. Your ego is your most powerful ally to keep you safe and alive. Your ego's intentions are always good, yet its strategies need to be revised to fit your adult life. The ego uses our fears—the fears of failure as much as the fears of success—as motivation to do all sorts of self-sabotaging things like hiding, doubting ourselves, procrastinating, punishing ourselves with negative self-talk, and illusionary expectations of perfection.

It's our job as female leaders to accept our ego as a devoted partner, team up with it, and turn the fears that trigger it into the energy to reach our goals and dreams!

Your Instant Insights...

- Know: Your ego is your committed servant to keep you alive and safe.

- Trust: The intentions of your ego are always good, yet its strategies are outdated as they stem from your early childhood programming.

- Lead with compassionate understanding for your ego, and your self-sabotaging habits will stop and your fears will turn into fuel for your dreams.

The Power of Acknowledgement

Über Woman Power Statement:
"I let go of resistance and drop all drama."

When we look at something, our senses transport the incoming data to our brain where it gets compared with old memories, against values, mixed with emotions, mulled over with some judgments, and checked to see if it is dangerous or pleasant for us. At the very end we come out with some kind of very personal opinion about what we saw or experienced, yet we think it is the correct objective representation of the external reality. It was the philosopher Jiddu Krishnamurti who said so wisely, "The ability to observe without evaluating is the highest form of intelligence." If you want to become a powerful leader, you have to train yourself in that ability.

Why? Our individual opinions separate us from others, they trigger emotions, they cause conflict, they create drama, they fix attention, and they make clear analytical thinking and complex decisions nearly impossible.

Listen to your staff members and team members, clients, and assistants more than you talk to them! When you talk and mention things you heard or observed, restrain yourself from personal judgment. Label things and events as simply as possible.

The German fairy tale from the Brothers Grimm called "Rumpelstiltskin" gives a powerful mystical example. In it a farmer's daughter makes a deal with a gnome who has the power to turn straw into gold so that she gets the prince. The gnome expects her to pay with her firstborn child. When he comes to request his payment, she begs him to leave the child with her. He makes her an offer: if she can figure out his secret name in three days, the child stays. She sends out her maids in all directions. One of her servants watches the gnome in a forest dancing around a fire and singing, "How great that no one knows my name is Rumpelstiltskin!" When the gnome comes to get his payment, the young queen says, "Rumpelstiltskin." Hearing his real name exposed, he becomes so angry that he tears himself apart and disappears forever. The point of this? When we are able to give things their name, their simple label without any story or drama, we have power over them!

Acknowledgment doesn't mean in this context to give compliments or to make things more positive than they are! It simply means going through your day and observing what is going on; it means dropping your need to make more out of it, and refraining from embellishing things with spices of drama here and there to make yourself more interesting in others' eyes. Stay neutral. Stay grounded. When you make a mistake, simply acknowledge it, clean up, and move on. When you see someone else making a mistake, label it simply as it is; don't add any blame or guilt or shame-inducing judgment! Talk neutrally about it without emotional charge. Experiment with this new way of communicating and being. Watch how much more energy you have at your disposal when your life becomes drama-free with the power of acknowledgment!

Your Instant Insights...

- Know: The highest form of human intelligence is observation without judgment.

- Trust: Tell it like it is, and all drama evaporates.

- Lead by acknowledging everything and everyone just as it is. By doing so, you will enjoy a sense of completion and the freed-up energy for more results you just created!

The Power of Self-Care

Über Woman Power Statement:
"I love my body, nurture my inner child, rest and play daily."

Most women agree quickly that health is the foundation to enjoying life fully, yet rarely do they connect the importance of health, their fitness level, and therefore their energy level with their performance level as a leader! As the overused metaphor from flight attendants says, "Put your oxygen mask on yourself first before helping others." How will you lead with power, clarity, and grace when you are sleep-deprived, irritable, and low on energy?

Since the early '80s, heart attacks, considered a "man's disease" in the past, have killed more women than men. This is correlated to the increased stress of high-powered positions in the corporate world and is considered one of the prices women pay for breaking through outdated glass ceilings. Caught up in patterns of perfectionism and fighting for proof they can be and do what in the past was considered only available for men, women became super women, burning themselves out in the process. Committed to functioning in an inhumane world—even for the men who created it—women pushed themselves beyond the limits of what is healthy for their bodies, minds, and spirits.

Analysis of high-performing athletes and artists shows a fascinating pattern: instead of "going, going, going" until they break down, exhausted (which is the pattern of most professional, high-achieving women in business), top performers follow a rhythm of a ninety-minute, totally focused work/training interval followed by ten minutes of rest, and then a new cycle starts.

The importance of eight hours of good, quality sleep (and in times of stress, even more) is widely documented. More and more companies allow their staff to use "sleep eggs" in designated, quiet, dark corners to get twenty-minute power naps during lunch breaks or in the late afternoon.

Hip, young Silicon Valley companies rediscover the importance of play for creativity, relaxation, and nurturing the human spirit by providing colorful, fun environments, soccer tables, Ping-Pong tables, basketball courts, and play rooms with cards and board games for their employees. We all have an inner child. When we neglect it and push ourselves for long periods of time, our inner little girl starts to feel neglected. It works through our subconscious mind and comes up with sabotaging strategies to get our attention. Mine, for example, is watching too much TV, even though work deadlines are sitting on my back or I'm super tired and should be in bed. No, my inner little girl wants some fun time and makes me watch a chick flick I've seen already five times while binging on chocolate, letting me gain back the pound I worked so hard all week to get off!

Talking in your own mind with your inner little girl while at work and checking in with her regularly is the best strategy to make her feel safe, validated, and cared for. Scheduling things to celebrate achievements ensures her collaboration for enduring long workdays. Allowing yourself to do one silly thing daily makes her happy. Maybe it is buying chewing gum at the gas station and blowing bubbles while you drive to work. Or wearing funny pink underwear no one can see under your business suit. Or buying yourself Tinker Bell pajamas. Or joining a Zumba class and dance once a week. You get the picture.

Sadly, exquisite self-care is for most female leaders the last thing they have on their plate. Their own business or corporate duties, work projects, husband, kids, family members, charity, household ... everything else comes first, and they come last. They don't want to think or feel they are selfish or guilty of vanity. Often they copy without awareness (because of loyalty) the way their mothers lived and worked, women who often followed a set of rules most women nowadays would consider completely outdated when consciously looked at!

How about you? Using a scale of 1 to 5 with 1 standing for "very bad/I forget it constantly," 3 standing for "half the time—I'm okay with that," to 5 standing for "I'm a master at that one. It's part of my daily healthy routine," rate yourself on the following listed items:

Suggested healthy habit:

- I go to bed daily at the same time.
- I make sure I get eight hours of uninterrupted sleep.
- I have a morning ritual just for myself where I nurture my body (e.g., one minute of stretching), my soul (e.g., ten minutes of meditating), and my mind (e.g., listening to positive empowerment audio while driving).
- I drink a glass of water every half hour.

- I get fresh air walking outside.

- I check in with my inner little girl when it gets intense or stressful and make sure she gets what she needs.

- I celebrate success.

- I take short breaks at least every ninety minutes.

- I eat healthy, fresh, nutritional food.

- I treat myself monthly to something special, like a massage or pedicure.

- I dedicate one evening per week to playtime with friends.

- I seek daily a few moments of stillness to reconnect with myself.

Congratulate yourself for every 4 or 5 you score. Be happy for the 3s and make a commitment to up-level the 1s and 2s! Choose one new healthy habit a week to work on, and when the first one is sustainably ingrained, choose the next one. Watch your energy level rise, your confidence level soar, and your results go up in all areas of your leadership and life!

Your Instant Insights...

- Know: A fit, healthy leader is a vibrant, charismatic leader who draws people and resources to her and produces bigger results.

- Trust: Self-care is like putting the oxygen mask on yourself first. It's not a luxury; it's a necessity!

- Lead with exquisite self-care for yourself as your highest priority so that you can then be your best for everyone else.

The Power of Projection

Über Woman Power Statement:
"I joyfully claim 100% responsibility as a creative being."

The human brain is full of biases and blind spots when it comes to our perception. We often perceive things to be real that aren't, despite the evidence and scientific proof at our disposal! Ask bystanders at a big traffic intersection after a car accident what they observed. If you ask twelve people, you'll get twelve different stories. They might overlap partially, yet they can sometimes completely contradict each other. Sadly, people can become pretty righteous about what they think they remember correctly, even though neuroscience has proven that there is no such thing as "objectively stored" memory.

Memory is fluid; it changes over time inside your subconscious mind. It doesn't just get "pulled out" with the same details of information your brain stored away a few months or years ago. No, while you extract it, you recreate that memory, which makes remembering a creative act!

As leaders we have to remind ourselves about that! For example, you have an argument with someone who didn't do something you wanted to get done, and that person remembers the way you explained your order differently than you do. Who is right? Probably neither.

When you have a person in your work environment—colleague or client—with whom you had a bad encounter, you store that as a memory. Every time you meet this person afterwards, you recall that memory, adding your own commentary to it and projecting it with your accompanying judgment (e.g., "This woman is annoying, unreliable, and hard to deal with."). This projection turns into an expectation that this person will indeed react in such a way that it proves your memory to be right. Thinking and feeling this projected expectation while going into the meeting with this person causes you to behave in a certain way. Think about it! How do you move toward someone, how do you stretch out your arm to shake hands, how do you look into their eyes, how tense are the muscles in your face, shoulders, and chest when you think, "This person is not reliable"? Are you hesitant? Maybe you turn your chest an inch away and don't show your full front? Do you pull your handshake back quickly? Maybe you can't really look into their eyes? The point is that your facial expressions, your gestures, and your muscle tension will speak louder than your words. That all happens with the speed of light and without your conscious awareness!

How do you think the other person will feel and react to you? We all have in our brain different classes of neuro cells. One class is called mirror-neurons because they function like a mirror. They allow us to feel what someone else close to us is feeling. They analyze all the data coming in through our senses to create a representation of the other person in our brain. They are one of the most important cells for human learning and enable us to develop empathy. When a very young baby smiles at the moment an excited grandma leans over the crib, the grandma yells excitedly, "My granddaughter just smiled at me!" However, she is wrong; a baby doesn't smile. Its mirror-neurons simply make it mimic what it sees! When you go out with a bunch of friends and the first person lifts their wine or beer glass toward their lips, suddenly the whole group around the table does it. During a board meeting, when one person fights yawning, suddenly everyone has the same issue. Our mirror-neurons make us feel connected by mimicking in ourselves what everyone else is feeling.

Back to the previous scene where you enter the room projecting and expecting the other person to fit your prejudiced belief of "annoying, unreliable, and difficult to deal with," how will that person react? That's right. Her mirror-neurons will analyze your body language, feel your hesitancy in her own body, and react accordingly, which means her feedback to you will prove your projection to be right! This will make you think: "I knew it. That person is really hard to connect with! You never know what she thinks. I can't trust her." Besides the disappointment you feel about people being like this, your brain also gives you the nice addictive sensation of "being right," confirming your judgment, which makes you feel safe and in control.

Is that person really annoying, unreliable, and hard to deal with? Maybe we will never know because we only met her through your perception filters and projections. Who made that woman behave like she did?

What if your power of projection is bigger than you ever thought it was?

What if everyone in your whole life acts out a script according to your expectations?

What if there is no such thing as an "objective world" and we all experience our own scripted Hollywood soap opera?

If you want different employees or clients (or even a new husband!), don't exchange the real people. Start by writing down your ideal vision of them. Then ask yourself: "What do I need to believe about them—which I then will project onto them—so that they, by acting according to my expectation, live out my envisioned ideal experience with them?" People will always live up to your expectations of them. Train yourself to go into every encounter being crystal clear about what you want to experience. Then expect that to happen by projecting your vision-aligned beliefs onto the situation and the people in it.

You are more powerful than you think you are. Use your creative power!

Your Instant Insights...

- Know: There is not one objective world. There are as many worlds as there are observers.

- Trust: You co-create your world moment by moment by moment.

- Lead by taking 100 percent ownership of everything you think, feel, and experience because what you experience is a result of your previous projections.

The Power of Commitment

Über Woman Power Statement:
"I trust my decisions and receive the support of the universe."

As a human being, you have to make thousands of decisions every day. Most of them are subconscious and tiny: do I lift my right leg out of bed first or my left one? Ingraining habits is one way your brain saves energy and reduces the number of exhausting decisions. A habit is a pattern of thinking, feeling, and acting that is run by your subconscious mind. Yes, you can break and change it with conscious willpower, yet if you have ever been on a diet or wanted to go more often to the gym, you know how hard that is. When you are tired or stressed, your subconscious behavioral patterns will always win!

As a leader, you have to make conscious decisions, sometimes about very complex things, and you are often responsible for their effect not only on you but on a lot of people and the bottom line. If you are a woman with a so-called "type A personality," you probably are used to making decisions fast and don't waste time doubting them. For most women that is not the case! A lot of healthy, energetic, professional women struggle with one (or several) of the following very common decision-making resistance patterns:

- **Codependency:** takes on too much responsibility for people in her environment, which is not hers to take on

- **People pleasing**: makes the decision more difficult and complex as she tries to please a lot of people with opposing interests

- **Perfectionism:** fails to act when she can't be 100 percent certain it will be perfect, which is rarely the case

- **Control issues:** the layers of unknown around the decision process and its consequences are too many and her fear of losing control stops her

- **Fear of failure:** believes that failure will have unbearable consequences, like losing control or approval

- **Fear of success:** could be loyalty issues around outshining someone or the fear of visibility, which undermines their safety

If you find several apply to you, don't judge yourself negatively! I had them all despite being a type A personality; I made decisions fast in the past, yet all hell broke loose afterwards for me!

When you look up the meaning of "commitment," you find a lot of different definitions. For me it means this: You are all in, 100 percent. No looking back, just forward. It shows in a discipline of focus, productive thinking, feeling, and acting accordingly.

You can gain the power of commitment with these five steps:

1. Be honest about your own decision-making pattern.

2. Get professional help, or ask a friend to be an accountability buddy to overcome those patterns that don't serve you any longer.

3. Use a "commitment journal" to write down how you feel before you make an important decision, while you make it, and afterwards.

4. Take note of what happens in the hours and days after you make a commitment!

Expect synchronicities, resources, and people to show up!

5. After you make a decision, train yourself to stay away from self-doubt. Self-doubt about a decision is a fireproof way to drive yourself nuts! Stop it!

The power of commitment not only attracts surprising resources and supports from the universe, you also exude more energy and charisma, which makes it easier for others to buy into your plans and follow you.

Your Instant Insights...

- Know: Indecisiveness is self-torture.
- Trust: Honesty is the key that unveils the decision you already made.
- Lead by committing fully, which will move providence in your favor.

The Power of Emotion Management

Über Woman Power Statement:
"I honor my emotions by choosing how to feel."

For most people, their own emotions are an undeniable reality. They treat whatever they feel as the only possible reality. For example, when they feel sad they believe whatever triggered that emotion is truly a sad event. Or if someone made them feel angry, they think that person is truly wrong and they are right to feel this way. People think there is a cause-and-effect connection between external situations and how they feel, meaning they couldn't feel differently—the external situation made them feel that way and it is outside their own control.

What if this were a misconception and far away from the truth?

What if external things like events and people are just triggers and never a true cause for anything going on emotionally inside you?

Imagine you are sitting in a restaurant waiting for your date to show up. You fill your time watching other couples sitting around you. It is a lovely, very hot summer night, and suddenly the five couples around you show a similar scene: the man says something, the woman throws a glass of water in his face, and his face and suit get wet. These are the facts, and they are all the same for each couple.

Yet now you can observe something interestingly different at each table: The first man stands up, angry and shouting some nasty words to the woman before he walks out of the restaurant. The second man laughs and stays in his seat. The third man stutters "I'm sorry" several times while wiping the water off with a napkin before he finally mumbles an excuse and disappears to the restroom. The fourth man pulls out his business card in exchange for hers so that he knows where to send the invoice from his dry cleaner for his damaged suit. The fifth man smiles brightly, leans forward, and kisses his woman lovingly. How is that possible? Same facts. Same "true reality." Yet five different reactions express five different emotions, from anger, humor, embarrassment, and cynicism to romantically aroused.

Human free will is present in the short time gap between the external triggers entering our awareness and our subconscious mind administrating an old preprogrammed automatic response pattern of feelings and actions. As a leader, you have to train yourself to become present to those micro-moments that determine whether you either fall into the trap of reacting automatically or are able to consciously choose a different, maybe more appropriate and goal-aligned response.

In our culture, we have two standard responses to how we manage our emotions: we either suppress them or express them. Suppressing them is often the choice we believe is safer or politer or expected of us, yet it hurts us, destroys our relationships, and undermines our authenticity, integrity, and health. Expressing them can escalate situations, igniting dramas and hurting others. In teams, they often waste a lot of energy, attention, and time. They hurt the bottom line of companies and businesses.

Only a few people know there is a third way: releasing what you feel, simply letting go of it, letting the chemical molecules that the feeling consists of run their course through your bloodstream and get disintegrated by your breathing, sweating, and other bodily functions. Whatever you feel, it is just a bunch of neurons firing in your brain, producing a bunch of molecules that get sent off into your bloodstream. When you don't interfere with the process by reacting to it, judging what you feel, and then expressing or suppressing it, the whole creation is over in just a few moments.

Be an Über Woman who leads by understanding human emotionality with compassion for yourself and others. Avoid all the related yet completely unnecessary dramas as much as possible.

Your Instant Insights...

- Know: Emotions are not good nor bad— they simply are. Your free will resides in the gap between the external trigger, your body's physiological response, and your response to that with feelings and actions.

- Trust: The two most common ways of managing your emotions, expressing and suppressing, are not the best ways to deal with them. Releasing them is.

- Lead powerfully by managing your own emotions and orchestrating the emotions of others.

The Power of the Spoken Word

Über Woman Power Statement:
"I change my story, stop hiding, and share my truth."

Even though I am writing in the year 2016 and the women's liberation movement has made huge strides in the last 100 years on the legal front—from women's right to vote, equal pay, access to the same educational and institutional resources—this progress is not fully globally established. When it is time for women to speak up, there are still way too many cultures, fanatics, and family traditions that follow the paradigms, "A woman has to be attractive yet not heard" and "When men speak, a woman has to stay quiet."

Even though most men and women consciously believe that a woman has the same right and the same power to speak up, share her truth, and lead through her words, in our subconscious mind we are still programmed with outdated stereotypes, role models, and collective memories from 7,000 years of patriarchal history! We might believe without being aware of it that it's not appropriate for a woman to stand out and speak up, or we believe it is not safe!

When a woman does speak up, she encounters the bias in her listeners' brains! When a woman and a man say the same thing as professional leaders, they are perceived—still—as saying something different! When a man talks a lot, his perceived status goes up. When a woman speaks a lot, her perceived status stagnates or even goes down. She simply gets disliked.

A lot of education and conscious rewriting of the stories we share about successful women are still needed to break the old stereotypes and cultivate a fair and equal perception of men and women's performances. Until then, every individual woman who wants to lead has to acknowledge her own subconscious fears. She needs to reassure her own ego that she is safe to speak up and that she will not get killed or lose her job or her husband when she does. Women now leave universities and colleges with higher degrees in higher quantities than men. Individual companies, the economy, and society at large miss out on their brilliance, strengths, and genius if women don't stop hiding and start sharing their unique perspectives and solutions for the world's problems.

Female leaders can train themselves to adopt the following healthy, confidence-strengthening habits that will help them embrace the power of the spoken word:

1. Allow themselves to interrupt others when their passion or the situation demands it without feeling guilty

2. Claim their own ideas and do not allow men to run with them under false pretense

3. Work on their full belly breathing and voice volume to project strongly and loudly when speaking to groups

4. Ground themselves more often by standing with their feet shoulder width apart, toes pointing outwards, imagining growing roots into the earth from under their feet, laying their hands briefly on their belly/ the solar-plexus, and imagining to speak from there versus just from their throat

5. Embrace numbers and facts to underline their stories

6. Stop waiting to speak up until they have 80 percent of the proof that they are right, and be inspired by men who voice their

opinion already with only 20 percent of the proof

7. Stop any negative self-dialogue and become the biggest internal cheerleader they can be

8. Imprint themselves with the belief "I'm enough"

9. Stop comparing themselves with men or other women and create alliances and collaborations with other powerful women, lifting each other up

10. Celebrate the sensual joy of feeling powerful when speaking their truth.

Your Instant Insights...

- Know: Hiding hurts yourself and others.
- Trust: You have a voice and a message the world needs to hear.
- Lead as if no woman ever got killed for speaking up.

The Power of Intuition

Über Woman Power Statement:
"I'm a clean channel for divine guidance. I receive, trust, and act."

In ancient times, all oracles were female (e.g., the oracle of Delphi in Greece whose temple inscription read "Know yourself!"). Sadly, the famous Greek fortune-teller Cassandra suffered from the curse so many modern female executives suffer too inside their corporate environments: she was not listened to or taken seriously.

Several thousand years of patriarchal cultural indoctrination has trained women to doubt their own inner wisdom. Women are used to listening to their father and other male authorities. Their own mother often ends up as an authority figure that they fight to outgrow and prove wrong. Yet more and more women discover that simply following the footsteps of their male (sometimes female) mentors and advisors doesn't necessarily work for them. More and more "super women" discover that the perfect blueprints of success that worked for their male peers don't often fit their own worldview and values. When they attempt to build their careers and lead with strategies they got from the outside, they often find themselves feeling inauthentic and out of integrity.

The courageous ones started asking themselves these questions: What if I stop listening to everyone else and start listening to myself? What if the answer is *not* another coach, mentor, guru, or training? What if the answer is getting truly still, going inward, asking, and receiving?

Yes, what if?

I can honestly say I was a high-achieving, yet stressed-out perfectionist, wanting-to-please-everyone "super woman." Yet the stress dropped away like dried-out leaves from a tree in autumn. The need to please everyone in order to fit in everywhere vanished.

The pressure to make things perfect before sharing them with the public evaporated.

When? The moment I finally stopped listening to others and started listening to my inner guidance.

Out of inner silence the Über Woman can emerge.

The path to trusting and having confidence in oneself and a productive relationship with your inner guidance, which we call "intuition," is not easy but it is learnable. It starts with Über Women Power #4: Ego-Love, which means you have to remind yourself that it is safe for you to know. Historically, women got punished too often for knowing things they were not supposed to know. So step one is: know it's safe to know.

Secondly, you have to nurture being a clean, empty channel for your inner wisdom to come through. Über Women Power #6: Self-Care! You don't need to believe in a divine power or any religious god to know from experience that intuition works. When asked what their biggest asset is for making the right decisions fast, most male CEOs say, "my gut instinct," which is just the male version of saying "my intuition." In order for you to hear it clearly, you need to lower your stress level and turn your inner-mind chatter down. There are countless ways to do this: sports, walking in nature, yoga, meditating, daydreaming, doing nothing, keeping white space in your calendar, staying offline for twenty-four hours, etc. Plus, having a small stomach that is not overfilled with heavy, fatty food, alcohol, sugar, and drugs supports your communication with your inner knowing voice.

How do you know you truly hear your intuition and not your ego's fears or other people's expectations yelling at you inside your own brain? There are indicators that distinguish your inner wise voice from all the other voices talking to you:

- It calms you down.
- It soothes you.
- It encourages you.
- It is optimistic.
- It strengthens you.
- It speaks highly of you.
- It empowers you.
- It speaks gently.
- It is patient.
- It is compassionate.
- It is sometimes metaphorical.
- It is sometimes mystical.
- It makes you feel better when you hear it.

The opposite kind of voice that creates stress; triggers fear; weakens you; embarrasses you; threatens you; pressures you; rushes you; is negative or pessimistic, cold, outright mean, judgmental, or very loud; and makes you feel worse when you hear it is *not* your intuition talking.

Thirdly, you need to act upon your intuition. That will strengthen your relationship with it and your confidence in yourself and its power.

Here is an important yet crucial detail: when you have an inner dialogue with your intuition and ask clear, specific questions, make sure you stay emotionally unattached to the outcome! As soon as you're attached emotionally to a specific outcome, it's your ego kicking in, trying to force the answer and results into existence.

When you open up to be guided by your own inner guidance system, leading becomes effortless, and you become an independent Über Woman!

Your Instant Insights...

- Know: You know, and it is safe for you to know.

- Trust: The cleanliness of your channel and the quality of your questions define the quality of the answers you get.

- Lead your team with your own personal advisor: your own trusted and trained intuition.

The Power of Unconditional Love

Über Woman Power Statement:
"I know my essence is love, peace, and freedom."

"Love" is a word you rarely hear inside corporate or business worlds, yet in recent years the zeitgeist demands more and more often that we do what we love doing and make money with that in order to find true happiness and meaning. This expectation, like the romantic one when it comes to "couple's love," assumes that love is "just there" when you are at the "right time" meeting the "right person" or doing the "right job." This paradigm of love is not supportive of your evolution into an Über Woman, your leadership success, or your happiness in your love life! This "love falls from the sky" paradigm gives the power to coincidences and circumstances; it does not put it into your hands.

I invite you to consider a radically different paradigm of love that has little to do with emotions, romance, and the coincidence of the "rightness" of all parts involved.

Consider this: Love is a conscious, creative act you choose.

- You choose to love.
- You choose to love yourself.
- You choose to love what you are doing in any given moment, independent of how you think that activity makes you feel.
- You choose to love the person in front of you, independent of how you think this person makes you feel.

True love is unconditional, or it is something else, such as attraction, hormones, obsession, duty, obligation, or a survival strategy—a dead-end street you believed had no alternative for you.

The ability to love and to lead from love is based on the following self-image: you consider yourself a free, fully responsible, peace-seeking woman and not a victim or an irresponsible woman addicted to drama.

Leading with unconditional love becomes possible when you have integrated all the other eleven Über Women Powers: when you have trained yourself to release emotions and emotional charge on your attention, and when you widened the gap between external input and your own reactions to make use of your free will. Leading as an Über Woman is a satisfying love affair!

Your Instant Insights...

- Know: Love is not like a virus you catch in the right moment with the right person or the right activity.

- Trust: Love is a conscious, creative act for you to choose.

- Lead with unconditional love and reap results that feel like magic.

Acknowledgements

Nothing worthwhile can be accomplished alone.

I want to acknowledge my mother who, traumatized by the Second World War as a child, is the source for my life's purpose to empower women to be able to live an uncompromised life. Thank you, Mom and Dad, for your deep love and confidence in me. You both did an amazing job!

Thank you, Peter, my beloved husband and biggest delight of my life for the 16 years together. You never get tired discussing with me the concepts I share in this book and arguing over fine yet important distinctions. No one understands me better than you do.

Thank you, Dianne, my beloved mother-in-law, for visiting us from New Zealand while I was finishing this book. Thank you for helping me cut out the "word waste" from the book, clean it up, and get it ready for submission.

Thank you, Robbin Simons, CEO of Crescendo Publishing, for your trust in choosing me to be in the lineup of authors for the launch of this powerful and needed Instant Insights series. Your guidance and writing templates made this last-minute project doable and easy for me. Thank you to the rest of my team at Crescendo Publishing for editing the book while honoring my voice, making her stronger and clearer, and for designing such a beautiful cover, which makes me happy like a little girl when holding my book.

Thank you to all my amazing, gorgeous, female clients from the last eighteen years. You are my heroines, constantly challenging the established assumptions in corporations and in business, constantly reinventing yourselves, constantly thriving and longing for a better you and a better world! Working and learning with you made me grow into the Über Women Movement leader I am now.

Thank you, first-time reader, for your investment of money, time, and attention to the book and its messages that are so close to my heart. Without you, the book would be worthless and my message unheard. May you become an unleashed, unashamed, and unstoppable Über Woman!

About the Author

Sylvia Becker-Hill is known as The Lady with the Brain™ because of her background in neuroscience and her passion for helping people make their dreams possible by teaching them how to rewire their own brain and align their subconscious mind with their conscious goals.

Sylvia is an award-winning entrepreneur on both sides of the Atlantic, a sought-after pioneer, trainer, and speaker of the international coaching industry, and a corporate change management expert with a focus on leadership and conflict resolution. With experience as a former manager at German Telecom, her Fortune 500 clients range from automotive to pharmaceutical, banking, transportation, manufacturing, and consulting.

Over the past 18 years, Sylvia has been reinventing herself as a womenpreneur, her business, and her life several times successfully while moving from continent to continent and from state to state. She is a published author in Germany and the US and is currently working on her leadership book series: *Uncaged, Unleashed, Unashamed, Unstoppable.*

With a university degree in gender studies plus thousands of hours of coaching female executives and female business owners, she provides professional women with the empowerment and tools to "have it all" on their own terms without sacrificing their health, themselves, or their love lives.

Through her global women's empowerment business **Über** Women International Inc., Sylvia offers professional women:

- 1-to-1 VIP Coaching Days in which professional women reinvent themselves and integrate and overcome any self-sabotaging outdated habits
- Customized coaching packages for implementation of the VIP Days or for sustainable power-habits creation
- Small, elite, women's retreats based on her forthcoming books *Uncaged*, *Unleashed*, *Unashamed*, *Unstoppable* at beautiful, serene locations with spa amenities all over the world
- A one-year-long **Über** Women Power Leadership Training (in person and virtual) based on the twelve powers described in this book, which her clients appreciatively call "The Hogwarts-School of Leadership™"
- In the future, the **Über** Women Academy will offer, with a team of different faculty

members, a wide range of training and educational leadership programs

To apply for any of Sylvia's programs and schedule a "Next Step on the Über Woman Path-Discovery-Session" with her or one of her client-care team members go here:

http://www.ueberwomen.com/contact.html

Connect with the Author

Website:
www.UeberWomen.com

Email:
Sylvia@UeberWomen.com

Social Media:
Facebook: www.facebok.com/
SylviaBeckerHillFan

LinkedIn: https://www.linkedin.com/in/
sylviabeckerhill

Twitter: @SylBeckerHill

Instagram: sylviabeckerhill

Periscope: SylBeckerHill

Snapchat: Sylvia Becker-Hill

https://www.pinterest.com/beckerhill/

Google+: Sylvia Becker-Hill

Address:
2249 Warmlands Ave Vista 92084 CA/USA

About Crescendo Publishing

Crescendo Publishing is a boutique-style, concierge VIP publishing company assisting entrepreneurs with writing, publishing, and promoting their books for the purposes of lead-generation and achieving global platform growth, then monetizing it for even more income opportunities.

Check out some of our latest best-selling AuthorPreneurs at http://CrescendoPublishing. com/new-authors/.

About the Instant Insights™ Book Series

The *Instant Insights™ Book Series* is a fact-only, short-read, book series written by EXPERTS in very specialized categories. These high-value, high-quality books can be produced in ONLY 6-8 weeks, from concept to launch, in BOTH PRINT & eBOOK Formats!

This book series is FOR YOU if:

- You are an expert in your niche or area of specialty

- You want to write a book to position yourself as an expert

- You want YOUR OWN book – NOT a chapter in someone else's book

- You want to have a book to give to people when you're speaking at events or simply networking

- You want to have it available quickly

- You don't have the time to invest in writing a 200-page full book

- You don't have a ton of money to invest in the production of a full book – editing, cover design, interior layout, best-seller promotion

- You don't have a ton of time to invest in finding quality contractors for the production of your book – editing, cover design, interior layout, best-seller promotion

For more information on how you can become an *Instant Insights™* author,
visit **www.InstantInsightsBooks.com**

Made in the USA
San Bernardino, CA
01 June 2016